BIGGEST NAMES IN SPORTS

# VLADIMIR GUERRERO JR.

## BASEBALL STAR

by Alex Monnig



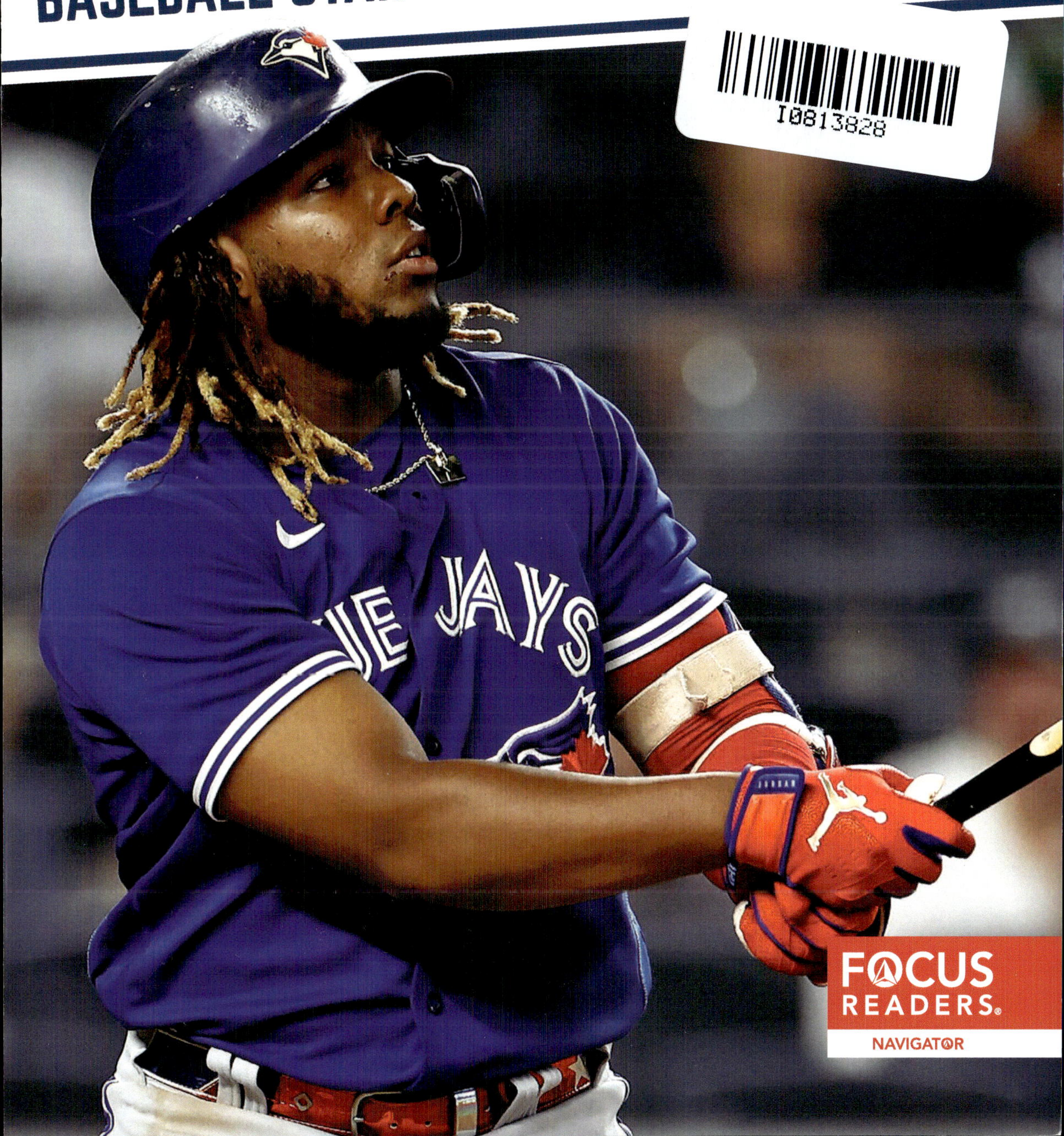


FOCUS READERS

NAVIGATOR

WWW.FOCUSREADERS.COM



Focus Readers is distributed by North Star Editions:
sales@northstareditions.com | 888-417-0195

Produced for Focus Readers by Red Line Editorial.

Photographs ©: Adam Hunger/AP Images, cover, 1; Kyodo/AP Images, 4–5; Gabriel Christus/AP Images, 7; Jack Dempsey/AP Images, 9; Paul Chiasson/The Canadian Press/AP Images, 10–11, 21; John Todd/AP Images, 13; Cliff Welch/Icon Sportswire, 15; Brian Westerholt/Four Seam Images/AP Images, 16–17; Mike Janes/Four Seam Images/AP Images, 18; Mark Blinch/The Canadian Press/AP Images, 22–23; John Minchillo/AP Images, 25; Julian Avram/Icon Sportswire, 27; Red Line Editorial, 29

**Library of Congress Cataloging-in-Publication Data**
Names: Monnig, Alex, author.
Title: Vladimir Guerrero Jr.: baseball star / by Alex Monnig.
Description: Lake Elmo, MN: Focus Readers, [2023] | Series: Biggest Names in Sports | Includes index. | Audience: Grades 4-6
Identifiers: LCCN 2022001996 (print) | LCCN 2022001997 (ebook) | ISBN 9781637392546 (Hardcover) | ISBN 9781637393062 (Paperback) | ISBN 9781637394076 (PDF) | ISBN 9781637393581 (eBook)
Subjects: LCSH: Guerrero, Vladimir, 1999---Juvenile literature. | Baseball players--Canada--Biography--Juvenile literature. | Toronto Blue Jays (Baseball team)--History--Juvenile literature. | All-Star Baseball Game--History--Juvenile literature. | Fathers and sons--Juvenile literature.
Classification: LCC GV865.G84 M66 2023 (print) | LCC GV865.G84 (ebook) | DDC 796.357092 [B]--dc23/eng/20220222
LC record available at https://lccn.loc.gov/2022001996
LC ebook record available at https://lccn.loc.gov/2022001997

Printed in the United States of America
Mankato, MN
082022

# ABOUT THE AUTHOR

Alex Monnig is a freelance writer from St. Louis, Missouri. Since graduating from the University of Missouri, Alex has covered sporting events around the world, including the Olympic Games, Rugby World Cup, Commonwealth Games, and more. He now lives in Sydney, Australia.

# TABLE OF CONTENTS

CHAPTER 1

# ALL-STAR PERFORMANCE

The whole baseball world was watching Vladimir Guerrero Jr. The Toronto Blue Jays first baseman was playing in the 2021 All-Star Game. No other games were happening that day. So, fans had only one place to go for baseball.

Guerrero stepped up to the plate in the third inning. He was playing for the

**Vladimir Guerrero Jr. takes a mighty swing at the 2021 All-Star Game.**

American League (AL). The AL had a 1–0 lead over the National League (NL). Corbin Burnes, one of baseball's best pitchers, was on the mound.

Guerrero stood up straight and held his bat high. On the first pitch, Guerrero took a big swing. He wanted to crush the ball. But he missed. The next pitch was outside the **strike zone**, and Guerrero let it go.

On the third pitch, Burnes threw a **slider**. Guerrero swung hard. And this time, he connected. Guerrero blasted the ball deep into left field. Burnes's jaw dropped. NL shortstop Fernando Tatís Jr. put his hands on his head. Fans watched

Guerrero watches the ball fly out of the park during the 2021 All-Star Game.

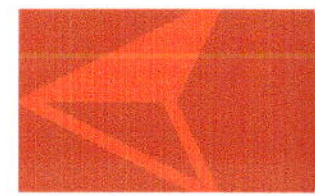

in amazement as the ball flew out of the park. It landed 468 feet (143 m) away from home plate.

The home run made the game 2–0. It also helped Guerrero win the All-Star

Game Most Valuable Player (MVP) Award. He was only 22 years old. That made him the youngest player to ever win the award. The All-Star Game doesn't count in the standings. For that reason, some fans say the game doesn't mean anything. But for Guerrero it did. Winning the MVP Award was a dream come true.

## LIKE FATHER, LIKE SON

**Vladimir Guerrero Jr.'s father also played in the major leagues. And just like his son, he hit a home run in the All-Star Game. It happened in 2006. The Guerreros became only the third father-son duo to hit All-Star Game homers. The first to do it were Ken Griffey Sr. and Ken Griffey Jr. The second pair was Bobby Bonds and Barry Bonds.**

Guerrero celebrates after winning the 2021 All-Star Game MVP Award.

Guerrero had shown flashes of potential during his career. His All-Star performance proved he was becoming a superstar.

Expos
Expos

# CHAPTER 2

# FOLLOWING IN DAD'S FOOTSTEPS

Vladimir Guerrero Jr. was born in Montreal, Quebec, on March 16, 1999. His father, Vladimir Sr., played Major League Baseball (MLB). He was an outfielder for the Montreal Expos.

In the summers, Vladimir Jr. traveled with his dad. He went to his father's games. During the rest of the year,

**Three-year-old Vladimir Guerrero Jr. joins his father on the field during a 2002 game with the Montreal Expos.**

Vladimir Jr. grew up in the Dominican Republic. That's where he learned how to play baseball.

He was happiest when playing baseball with his brothers and cousins. He learned the game on dusty fields outside his hometown of Nizao. His uncle Wilton Guerrero coached him. Wilton was also an MLB player.

## VLAD THE DAD

**Vladimir Guerrero Sr. played 16 seasons in the major leagues. Most were with the Montreal Expos and Los Angeles Angels of Anaheim. Guerrero was a great hitter. He also had a powerful arm in right field. Guerrero was a nine-time All-Star. In 2018, he became a member of the Hall of Fame.**

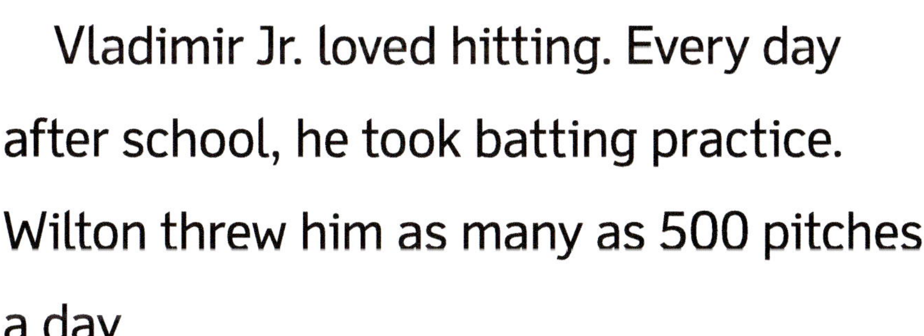

Wilton Guerrero makes a play during a 2004 game with the Kansas City Royals.

Vladimir Jr. loved hitting. Every day after school, he took batting practice. Wilton threw him as many as 500 pitches a day.

Before long, many **scouts** started hearing about Vladimir Jr.'s incredible skills. So, they traveled to the Dominican

Republic to watch him. The scouts were amazed. Vladimir Jr. was just 15 years old. But he was getting hits against older pitchers who were already with minor league teams. His huge home runs caught everyone's attention.

But it wasn't just the hitting that impressed the scouts. Vladimir Jr. also showed patience. He didn't swing at pitches outside the strike zone.

Scouts for the Toronto Blue Jays spoke to Vladimir Jr.'s parents. They invited the young slugger to private workouts. The scouts wanted to get to know him better. They learned about his love for the game and his fun-loving attitude.

Sixteen-year-old Vladimir Guerrero Jr. practices with a minor league team in 2015.

The Blue Jays scouts were very impressed. On July 2, 2015, the team signed 16-year-old Vladimir Jr. to a **contract**. It was official. He was a professional baseball player.

# CHAPTER 3

# MINOR LEAGUES, MAJOR SKILLS

The Toronto Blue Jays thought Vladimir Guerrero Jr. could be a star. But like most baseball players, he started his career in the minor leagues. There, young players improve their skills. There are several different levels of minor league baseball. Players move up to higher levels as they get better.

**Guerrero swings for the fences during a 2016 minor league game with the Bluefield Blue Jays.**

Guerrero fields the ball for the Lansing Lugnuts in 2017.

In 2016, Guerrero began at the lowest level. He was only 17 years old. Still, he became an All-Star with the Bluefield Blue Jays. By 2018, Guerrero had already climbed up to Triple-A. That's the highest level of the minor leagues.

Guerrero impressed lots of people along the way. In those three years, he had a .331 **batting average**. He also had more walks than strikeouts. That meant he was not only a great hitter. He was also good at recognizing balls and strikes.

When Guerrero was 19 years old, he had the highest batting average in the minor leagues. Baseball experts were calling him one of the best hitting **prospects** ever. They loved how he could hit home runs to any part of the field.

The 2018 season started in a special way for Guerrero. The Blue Jays played a **spring training** game in Montreal. The game took place in Olympic Stadium. That's where Guerrero's father had played his first eight seasons. However, the Montreal Expos didn't exist anymore. They had become the Washington Nationals.

Guerrero wore his dad's No. 27 for the game. The fans in Montreal loved him. As he walked to the plate, many fans stood and cheered. The score was 0–0. There were two outs in the bottom of the ninth inning. On the second pitch of the at-bat, Guerrero launched a home run to win the game. His teammates waited at home plate to celebrate. The crowd went wild.

Guerrero celebrates his game-winning home run during a 2018 exhibition game in Montreal.

Guerrero went on to become the 2018 Minor League Player of the Year. It was clear that he was ready for the next step in his career.

GUERRERO JR.
27

CHAPTER 4

# BECOMING A SUPERSTAR

Vladimir Guerrero Jr. had proved that he belonged in the major leagues. So, in 2019, the Toronto Blue Jays added him to the team. Fans expected a lot from the **rookie**. He had been amazing in the minor leagues. And his dad was a Hall of Famer. Many thought Guerrero would be an instant superstar.

Guerrero hits the ball during his first major league game.

Unfortunately for Blue Jays fans, that wasn't the case. In his first two seasons, Guerrero didn't show the same hitting skills he'd had in the minors. The speed of the game was different. He struggled in the field, and he was out of shape. He got tired over the longer MLB season.

But there were still some highlights. Guerrero put on a show at the 2019 Home

## MANY NAMES

**Vladimir Guerrero Jr. has many nicknames. He is known as Vlad Jr., Vladito (which means "Little Vlad" in Spanish), and Vladdy. He is also known by the term Plákata. This word comes from slang used in the Caribbean. It refers to the bat making solid contact on the ball, resulting in a long home run.**

Guerrero pumps up the crowd after crushing a home run at the 2019 Home Run Derby.

Run Derby. He set a record with 91 home runs in the contest.

After his rookie year, the Blue Jays asked Guerrero to lose weight. They also moved him from third base to first base.

However, his problems continued in 2020. Guerrero apologized to his teammates and promised to do better. And he did. In 2021, he showed up to spring training 42 pounds (19 kg) lighter.

The hard work paid off. Guerrero had a breakout season. In fact, he nearly won the Triple Crown. That's when a player leads the league in home runs, runs batted in (RBI), and batting average. Guerrero tied for the MLB lead with 48 homers. That was a record for a player under the age of 23.

Guerrero was also selected for the All-Star Game, where he earned MVP honors. And he finished second in

Guerrero trots around the bases after hitting a home run in 2021.

AL MVP voting. Guerrero was living up to expectations. Blue Jays fans couldn't wait to see what came next.

# VLADIMIR GUERRERO JR.

- Height: 6 feet 2 inches (188 cm)
- Weight: 250 pounds (113 kg)
- Birth date: March 16, 1999
- Birthplace: Montreal, Quebec
- Minor league teams: Bluefield Blue Jays (2016); Lansing Lugnuts (2017); Dunedin Blue Jays (2017, 2018, 2019); GCL Blue Jays (2018); New Hampshire Fisher Cats (2018); Buffalo Bisons (2018, 2019)
- MLB team: Toronto Blue Jays (2019–)
- Major awards: MLB All-Star (2021); All-Star Game MVP (2021)

Montreal
Toronto
Manchester
Lansing
Buffalo
Bluefield
Dunedin

## FOCUS ON

# VLADIMIR GUERRERO JR.

*Write your answers on a separate piece of paper.*

**1.** Write a paragraph explaining the main ideas of Chapter 3.

**2.** Why do you think Guerrero struggled in his first two MLB seasons?

**3.** Which team did Vladimir Guerrero Sr. play for?

- **A.** Washington Nationals
- **B.** Toronto Blue Jays
- **C.** Montreal Expos

**4.** In the 2018 spring training game, why did the Montreal fans cheer as Guerrero walked to the plate?

- **A.** They cheered loudly for every player no matter what.
- **B.** They had fond memories of Guerrero's father.
- **C.** They knew he was about to hit a game-winning home run.

*Answer key on page 32.*

# GLOSSARY

**batting average**

The number of hits a player has divided by the number of times at bat.

**contract**

An agreement to pay someone a certain amount of money.

**prospects**

Players who are likely to be successful in the future.

**rookie**

A professional athlete in his or her first year.

**scouts**

People whose jobs involve looking for talented young players.

**slider**

A pitch that moves down and away from the batter.

**spring training**

A time when players get ready for the upcoming season.

**strike zone**

The area over home plate that is above the batter's knees and below the batter's shoulders.

# TO LEARN MORE

## BOOKS

Doeden, Matt. *It's Outta Here!: The Might and Majesty of the Home Run*. Minneapolis: Lerner Publications, 2021.

Gitlin, Marty. *Great Baseball Debates*. Minneapolis: Abdo Publishing, 2019.

Kortemeier, Todd. *Fernando Tatís Jr.: Baseball Star.* Lake Elmo, MN: Focus Readers, 2023.

## NOTE TO EDUCATORS

Visit **www.focusreaders.com** to find lesson plans, activities, links, and other resources related to this title.

# INDEX



**Answer Key: 1.** Answers will vary; **2.** Answers will vary; **3.** C; **4.** B